Michelle Ru

Welcome to
the Club…

I'm sorry you're here.

Hope for grieving parents

Michelle Ruddell

Welcome to the Club—I'm Sorry You're Here

Michelle Ruddell

Table of Contents

Acknowledgements

In the twenty plus years since I joined this club, there have been many people who have contributed to this story. Some of our paths have not crossed in years, yet your support during those first days was vital.

To each club member I've met along the way, thank you for sharing your story and for what I have learned from you.

To my dear friend and encourager Reita Hawthorne, thank you for always asking, "What are you writing?" even when life was way too busy.

To my critique group, Chris, Jane, Linda, and Joye, thank you for reading through the heavy stuff. Thank you for making me a better writer.

To my family, thank you for not giving up on me and for always listening to my "I'm going to write a book" stories. See? It's finally happening!

Introduction

I'm a part of a club that no one wants to join. Initiation is involuntary. Members come from every nationality, religion, and social status. New arrivals are likely in shock, looking for answers from those who were inducted long ago. In this group there is strength from shared experience. Hope is found from veteran members who manage to function in their new normal. Entry to this tribe is gained through loss. Each unwilling participant has experienced an out-of-the-natural-order event. This club consists of parents who have endured the death of a child.

If you are a new addition to this club, I am sorry for your loss. May you gain hope, comfort, and perspective from those of us who have walked in your shoes.

The Short Version

If your loss is very recent, you may not be in much of a reading mood. Here are some things to hang on to in the here and now.

Words of encouragement:

- A new normal will surface.

- You can be happy again.

- There are others who have survived this heartbreak.

To do:

- Let people help.

- Cry when you want to cry.

- Trust God.

- Be gentle with yourself.

What Now?

"It's not supposed to happen this way. Parents are not supposed to bury their children." These words of agony poured from the heart of my friend's father-in-law. His son, age thirty-five, had been declared brain-dead after a stroke. The family had made the excruciating decision to withdraw life support. A few years later the memory of this man pacing the hallway of the hospital surfaced when my own son, age five, was killed in a car accident. I identified with the grieving father. My entire world was turned upside down. It surely wasn't supposed to happen this way.

What do we do when the unthinkable happens? What do we do now? Several years ago, I made a phone call to my friend Atha, a new member to this club that no one wants to join. I faced a dilemma. I wanted to speak to this grieving mom and tell her I understood, but I felt helpless to ease her pain. I prayed before I dialed her number. I asked God to give me the words to say.

"This is when we find out that all those things we said we believe about God are *really true*." I heard myself tell my grieving friend. "This is when we truly find out how faithful, how strong, and how capable God is."

The first days after my son died were surreal. Tasks that were usually done without thinking (like walking and breathing) required what seemed to be super-human effort. I had never experienced this kind of pain. I had no control over my emotions. Alongside deep sorrow, I dealt with shock and denial, accompanied by overwhelming fear. In the strangest juxtaposition came the peace of knowing God was in control. There was an underlying confidence that He would carry me through the hardest days of my life. I was surrounded by people who loved me. They made sure I ate and slept. I let them help. I was busy trying to walk and breathe.

My suggestion to parents new in this grief is to be patient and gentle with yourself. Put one foot in front of the other. Breathe in, breathe out. Let people help. Trust God to carry you through.

> *The LORD is close to the brokenhearted and saves those who are crushed in spirit.* Psalm 34:18

How We Got Here

There are many life events that lead to membership in this club that no one wants to join. My initiation came when my son died in a car accident. I have a friend who was inducted when her son died after a battle with cancer. A parent of a former student of mine was thrust into our ranks when her son died by suicide. Many parents enter this group when their children die before birth. Some families have the added burden of losing a child to a criminal act.

Though our avenues of admission are different, the sorrow and loss are the same. We all experience life-altering grief when we suffer the death of a child. Our world has been shaken. Normal has vanished. We can't undo what has been done. Nothing about joining this club makes sense. Becoming a member wasn't on anyone's agenda. We got here by circumstances beyond our control.

Although induction into this society makes us feel isolated and alone, you may be surprised to find many of our number in your acquaintance. Most don't advertise their affiliation but will identify themselves once they know you have joined.

Two are better than one, because they have a good return for their labor: If either of them falls down, one can help the other up. Ecclesiastes 4:9-10

The Same but Different

On a recent Sunday morning, I spoke with a fellow member of the club. We share an experience that forever affects our *normal*. She lost her son to cancer when he was six; mine died in a car accident at age five.

We exchanged Easter greetings and gave quick life updates. I remarked how much her two surviving sons have grown and shared the ages of my now-adult daughters. I told her my Matthew would now be thirty-one. Her Paul would be seventeen.

The conversation took a quick turn to what our boys would be like as grown-ups. It's hard to imagine our forever children as adults. I apologized for bringing up sad thoughts, but my friend is like me. She loves talking about her child. Although he is not here, she's still his mom.

I remember talking to her not long after her son died. We spent a few minutes comparing losing a child after a lengthy illness to losing a child unexpectedly in an instant. She had time to "prepare" (if that is at all possible). She watched her child suffer. She and her husband exhausted every possible treatment in one attempt after another to find a cure for their son. I'm sure their hopes rose with each new method, only to plummet when the cancer returned. They knew for a time that their sweet Paul was going to die. On the other hand, my Matthew was gone in an instant. I had no warning, no chance to save him. I had no opportunity to say goodbye. I didn't watch my son suffer. I didn't have to stand by and see him endure painful medical procedures without being able to ease his suffering. We lived up until his last minute completely unaware that the time was short.

After weighing the similarities and differences of the way we each endured the death of our child, we concluded: *both ways stink!* One way is no better or worse than the other. The unnatural event of burying a child is painful. It is heart-wrenching. Neither of us would wish this trial on anyone.

"I have told you these things, so that in me you may have peace. In this world you will have trouble. But take heart! I have overcome the world." John 16:33

The Reality

My world stopped when I heard those heart-wrenching words, "Matthew didn't make it." The worst possible thing I could imagine was now reality. The first few days were spent surrounded by family and friends. The intense pain of the sudden loss was cushioned by the constant comfort of those around me. Several incidents that pierced the fog of denial and disbelief that this was really happening:

- ## **The Funeral Home**

My whole body hurt. My bones and muscles throbbed from the trauma of the car crash. My heart ached from the death of my son. My mind raced with concern for my husband who was clinging to life in the ICU. All those hurting parts struggled to keep going to protect my unborn daughter.

I took one slow, painful step after another into the room at the funeral home. The small white casket looked just like the one I had chosen from the pictures my dad showed me in the hospital. There lay my brown-eyed, brown-haired boy, his chubby hands folded across his chest. He would have loved the black and red wind suit my mom had picked out for him. "He's just not a suit-and-tie kind of kid," I told her.

Is this really happening? Are you sure he's not going to open his eyes, flash that smile, jump up, and take off running?

Instinctively I reached out and grasped his hand. That icy touch pierced my soul with reality: Matthew was gone.

The funeral home directors were waiting for me to decide if the casket would be open for the service. Our closest family and friends had already seen him. The best work of the staff couldn't completely mask the fact that my precious son had suffered massive head injuries. I decided that the lid should be closed. I wanted us all to remember that vibrant, energetic little boy as he was *before* the violent crash that took his life.

Brothers and sisters, we do not want you to be uninformed about those who sleep in death, so that you do not grieve like the rest of mankind, who have no hope. For we believe that Jesus died and rose again, and so we believe that God will bring with Jesus those who have fallen asleep in him. According to the Lord's word, we tell you that we who are still alive, who are left until the coming of the Lord, will certainly not precede those who have fallen asleep. For the Lord himself will come down from heaven, with a loud command, with the voice of the archangel and with the trumpet call of God, and the dead in Christ will rise first. After that, we who are still alive and are left will be caught up together with them in the clouds to meet the Lord in the air. And so we will be with

Michelle Ruddell

*the Lord forever. Therefore encourage one another with
these words.* 1 Thessalonians 4:13-18

• **Saying Good-bye**

In the altered-reality time warp of the first few days
after Matthew's death, my heart and my brain blasted a
phrase on repeat. Like the emergency broadcast
warnings on TV, all thought processes were interrupted
or drowned out by, "I didn't get to tell him goodbye."
My mom-brain was in full-throttle crisis mode. My
child had been hurt, had been taken to the hospital, and
had died. My job as his mother was to protect him and
to comfort him. I hadn't been able to do either. I had
failed him. He had passed from this life to the next
without any words or touch from me. I couldn't get
past that thought. I couldn't fix it for Matthew, and I
couldn't fix it for me. As often as I said the words,
"He's in Heaven. He's with Jesus. He's not suffering." I
could *not* resolve the idea that I didn't get to voice any
parting words to my son.

One night the sheer exhaustion overpowered the
dread of laying my head on the pillow. I fell into the
sleep of one whose physical and emotional resources
were depleted. While I was sleeping, I saw Matthew's
face and heard his voice. "Don't worry about me, Mom.
I'm okay."

When I awoke, the blaring, crisis-mode message had
stopped. I was still heartbroken. I was on the verge of
tears often, but my despair over not telling Matthew

goodbye was gone. The image of him dying alone had been replaced with the image of him at peace.

And the **peace** *of God, which transcends all understanding, will guard your hearts and your minds in Christ Jesus.* Philippians 4:7

• His Room

Days later, when I went home for the first time, I collided with my new reality. The brown-eyed, brown-haired boy who had been sliding down the driveway in his snow boots a few short days ago was dead. My live-wire kid who stopped mid-run that fateful morning to give me a hug and say, "I love you Mom," was gone. The crooked grin, the bubbly laugh, the chubby fingers; these were no longer part of my day. I couldn't see him. I couldn't hear him. I couldn't touch him.

Opening the door to his bedroom was like removing a band-aid. I opened it as slowly as I could, dreading the pain of yet another reminder that Matthew was gone. There was his bed, never to be slept in by him again. There were his Hot Wheel cars, lined up in a row on the floor waiting for his return. The room was his. Reminders of my bouncy, bubbly boy were everywhere. I shut the door. I didn't have to deal with those yet.

I remembered the story told by my mother's neighbor who had also lost a son. She said they left his room exactly as he left it for years. I could understand why. I also knew that in a few months we would have a new baby who would need that bedroom. There would need to be a change. That room would transform from Matthew's to Missy's. But that change wouldn't happen today.

> *"For I know the plans I have for you," declares the Lord, "plans to prosper you and not to harm you, plans to give you hope and a future."*
> Jeremiah 29:11

• **The Tree**

The bare, plastic tree stood in the living room long after Christmas. I didn't have the strength or the will to take it down. A few weeks before, Matthew had not-so-patiently waited while his dad and I put the tree together. We were all disappointed when we discovered we had no hooks for the ornaments. The decorating would have to wait until after the trip to Lubbock.

Now the tree stood, strangely out-of-place. Undecorated, with its appointed day past. I couldn't decorate it, and I couldn't take it down. Finally, some family members gently asked if they could take it down and put it away. I let them. I didn't watch. We gave that tree away before the next Christmas.

> *Be merciful to me, Lord, for I am in distress;*
> *my eyes grow weak with sorrow,*
> *my soul and body with grief.*
> Psalm 31:9

• His Classmates

In the months after the wreck, I seldom considered Matthew's classmates. I was occupied with my own grief, a husband recovering physically and emotionally, and the birth of our precious baby girl. At the end of the school year, I was given a copy of the yearbook for his elementary school. There was a full-page photo of my smiling, brown-eyed boy. His teacher told me that the boys and girls in the class had continued to talk about Matthew and include him in games. "It's Matthew's turn," she would hear them say as they paused and gave their not-forgotten classmate his chance.

As the years passed, I often struggled as I watched his peers grow up, play ball, and meet normal, everyday milestones. Seeing them reminded me of what I was missing. I was jealous of families who were not grieving like me.

As Matthew's classmates became teenagers, my feelings of loss intensified. From the day my nine-pound-four-ounce boy was born, I had dreamed of watching him play football. Now his peers were playing. My friends were football-moms. They were teaching their sons to drive and waiting up for them to come home from dates. I dreaded their senior year of high school. I wasn't sure how I could handle the celebration and recognition that would serve as a constant reminder of what I *didn't* have. I would be happy for the other moms, but I was sure my sadness would show through.

God knew my need and my heart. In his perfect timing, he moved the girls and me to a new job, a new school, and a new town just in time for that senior year. I was so busy adjusting to new *everything* that it took me a while to realize: The students I was teaching in my new job, the ones I was cheering for during Friday-night football and getting to know in the classrooms and hallways of the high school—they were the same age as my Matthew.

> *So I will restore to you the years that the*
> *swarming]locust has eaten,*
> *The crawling locust,*
> *The consuming locust,*
> *And the chewing locust,*
> *My great army which I sent among you.*
> *You shall eat in plenty and be satisfied,*
> *And praise the name of the* LORD *your God,*
> *Who has dealt wondrously with you;*
> *And My people shall never be put to shame*
> *Then you shall know that I am in the midst of Israel:*
> *I am the* LORD *your God*
> *And there is no other.*
> *My people shall never be put to shame.*
> Joel 2:25-27 NKJV

The Hardest Things

Not hearing his voice
Not seeing his smile
Wondering what he would look like, sound like, and
act like now.
Never seeing him with his sisters
Not being able to talk to him
Not being able to hold his hand
Not being able to hug him.
Wondering if I would be a grandmother by now.
These are the hardest things.

Heavenly Father,

Thank you for your faithfulness, strength, and comfort during these hard days. Thank you for your comfort as I write these words to share hope with others. Thank you for being close to the brokenhearted* and for being our refuge and strength. ** Thank you for the hope we have in Christ Jesus and the promise of a joyful reunion one day. May you be glorified in all things. Amen.

*Psalm 34:18
**Psalm 46:1

Moving Forward

My world had stopped while everyone else's kept spinning. As badly as I wanted to turn back time, it cruelly continued forward. Every minute seemed to take me further and further away from my beloved boy.

In those first few weeks at home, I looked and listened for my son. I hadn't found an off switch for my mom-mentality. It felt strange to not set his place at the table, but I still had to eat. It was weird to go to work without taking him to school, but it was necessary for me to keep my job. The car was quiet without him, but daily life required driving. The house didn't feel like home, but it was where I lived. I had to function in my grief.

I had received some valuable advice from a friend who cautioned me, "Be gentle with yourself." I remembered her words as I plodded through those early days. There were times when I did things differently if the familiar was too painful. For example, we had eaten at Matthew's favorite fast food restaurant the night before the wreck. I couldn't bring myself to eat there for months. At other times, routines were comforting. There were times we did things specifically because that's the way Matthew would have done it. What worked to get me through the day varied. What helped me sometimes didn't help my husband in his grief, or my parents in theirs. We learned to be patient with each other. Nothing about it was easy.

In time a new normal begins to emerge. The first laugh might catch you off guard. You may be surprised when you find yourself having a good time. Remember to be gentle with yourself. It is possible and permissible to enjoy things in life after the loss of a child. Being happy doesn't mean you don't miss them. Finding joy doesn't mean there's no sorrow. Sometimes the two co-exist in ways you had not thought of before.

Save me, O God,
for the waters have come up to my neck.
I sink in the miry depths,
where there is no foothold.
I have come into the deep waters;
the floods engulf me.
I am worn out calling for help;
my throat is parched.
My eyes fail,
looking for my God.
Psalm 69:1-3

Bitter or Better

"Times like these can make you bitter or better." The preacher's words hit home with me. I did not remember them from the service but had watched a recording some months later. There were moments where bitter was winning. It was easy to fall into self-pity and anger.

Losing a child is not fair. I had every right to feel those emotions. Those feelings were justified, but they were not beneficial for me. I finally understood the words of my dear friend Norma Brown when she said that sometimes even emotions I have a right to are "not a luxury I can afford."

Another friend, who had lost her husband unexpectedly at age thirty-five, offered wisdom regarding the stages of grief. "Some days you may experience them all in one day. At times you may go through them much more slowly. The key is not to get stuck in any one stage."

My parents' neighbor had unknowingly dared me to fight against being bitter. She had looked me in the eye days after my son's funeral and said, "You will never be happy again."

Her words made me angry. I asked God that very day to help me choose better over bitter. When I was tempted to wallow in self-pity or found myself angry at everything and everyone, I would remember her words. I would ask God for help. He heard my prayer every time. He was faithful to provide some way for me to focus on what was good.

> *Trust in the LORD with all your heart*
> *and lean not on your own understanding;*
> *in all your ways submit to him,*
> *and he will make your paths straight.*
> Proverbs 3:5-6

The Things People Say

"You are so *strong*. I don't know how you do it." This well-intentioned remark made me angry. On multiple occasions, I found myself struggling to reply in a civil manner. I didn't want to be *strong*. Was there another choice? Could I curl up in a corner and just quit? Could I turn back time and undo the worst thing that had ever happened to me? I certainly didn't *feel* strong. I could barely function. I was at a complete standstill while the rest of the world kept spinning. How on earth could these people think I was strong?

Membership in this club no one wants to join means you will hear a multitude of messages. Some will be helpful. Others will make you angry. A few will make no sense at all. A friend of mine whose infant died unexpectedly once told me she was going to write a book called, "What *Not* to Say to Someone Who Has Lost a Child." Some comments reported by veteran members of our ranks include:

- "Your child is in a better place." *I don't want my child any place but with me.*

- "I know how you feel." *No, you don't. Even if you've suffered a loss, each person grieves differently.*

- "Well, you can have other children." *Children are not interchangeable. I love my other children and grieve the loss of my son.*

- "God must have needed him (or her)." *I needed my child. Why would God take him or her away?*

- "Now you have an angel watching over you." *I want my child here with me.*

- "God has a plan." *I cannot grasp why the plan must include this. Is my faith not strong enough?*

- "All things work together for good…" *I cannot possibly see any good in this situation. This scripture is not helpful for grieving parents, especially when that grief is new.*

When inadequate words meet with inexpressible sorrow, the result can be unintentional hurt. Our emotions are already raw and close to the surface. Our world has been shaken and our normal forever altered. People are saying things that seem to make us feel worse instead of better.

While grieving parents are desperately grasping for something to make sense of their loss, those around them are just as desperately searching for words to relieve the hurt. The trouble is this: There are no words that will bring their loved one back. No magic phrase will ease or erase the pain that comes from the death of a child.

To you, the constituents of our cohort, I encourage patience with both the makers of these comments and with yourself as you react to them. In our grief we may perceive some statements as insensitive when, in fact, they were offered in a genuine attempt to comfort.

Sometimes words that make us angry or don't make sense can serve a purpose that we may not have considered. I was shocked when my parents' neighbor told me, "You will never be happy again." I left the room because I didn't want to hear anything else she had to say. Amid many strong emotions, I knew I did not want her words to be true. I prayed that God would help me to *not* be bitter and unhappy forever. In the very difficult days, weeks, and months that followed, when I was tempted to *stay* in self-pity and anger, I remembered her words and my prayer. She unknowingly provided the push for me to strive to be happy again.

Some messages you will hear from others will bring comfort and worthwhile advice. A friend of mine, whose husband died unexpectedly at age thirty-five, gave me permission to grieve in my own way when she said, "Don't let anyone tell you *how* to grieve." She assured me that each person deals with grief in his or her own way.

One member, Linda, reported that she was helped when a friend gave her a book called *Good Grief* by Granger E. Westberg. This short little book explains the stages of grief. In a time when life's *normal* is being redefined, it is reassuring to know that the feelings you are experiencing are part of the grief process.

Another club veteran, Tara, remembered being comforted when a friend told her it was okay to be sad and to cry. This representative of our group conveyed to Tara that it is possible to be a believer and to grieve. This message is important. Sometimes as Christians we think we must be stoic: If we just have enough faith, we will always be happy. That is contrary to the words of Jesus. He said, *"I have told you these things, so that in me you may have peace. In this world you will have trouble. But take heart! I have overcome the world."* John 16:33

As a new member of this club that no one wants to join, you will hear many messages. I am reminded of a phrase I heard frequently from some twelve-step friends regarding meetings. Attendees were encouraged to "take what you like and leave the rest." Some things people say will apply to you and be beneficial as you work through the grief process. Others may not be of any use to you. I encourage you to take what is helpful and leave the rest.

"Then young women will dance and be glad, young men and old as well. I will turn their mourning into gladness; I will give them comfort and joy instead of sorrow." Jeremiah 31:13

"Those who sow with tears will reap with songs of joy." Psalm 126:5

The Clouds Roll In

It sneaks up on me every year. Suddenly I notice the chill in the air and the chill in my soul. The breeze that makes me pull my sweater tight, the early darkness of the shorter days, and the smell of smoke from a neighbor's chimney are reminders to all my senses that the time of year is here. A cloud rolls over my soul as the sights and smells of late November awaken the part of my brain and my heart to the hardest season of my life.

Details that would normally be crowded out by new memories are etched into my mind because they were *lasts*. The first Thanksgiving in our new-to-us home was the *last* Thanksgiving with my son. The dollar-store-butterfly wind chime was his *last* birthday gift to me. The sight of him sliding down the barely icy driveway in his snow boots was the *last* time I'd see him play. As he raced through the living room, he stopped suddenly, wrapped his arms around me and squeezed me in the *last* hug I would ever get from him. As he looked up at me, I heard him say his *last* "I love you, Mom."

The change of seasons brings to the surface these precious, bittersweet memories. In the first few years after my son's death, this awakening of emotions was excruciating. My grief process was starting all over again. I wondered if I had made any progress at all. I dreaded that season and the approaching anniversary of the day that changed my life forever, December 5, 1992.

As the day rolled around each year, I tried to find a way to deal with the flood of feelings that I knew was coming. I tried to crowd out the grief. I scheduled as many activities as possible, dragging my poor daughters around shopping, eating out, going to movies, or bowling. Sheer exhaustion was better than being home where my mind had time to remember the grief.

I would also tell anyone who would listen how hard that day was going to be for me. For weeks I would warn my friends that I was going to have a rough time. I remember being very upset when my friends went on with their lives on that day. It was my grief, not theirs. My world had stopped, but theirs had not. It took me a long time to learn that just because these anniversary days were not a life-stopper for them, it didn't mean they didn't care about me.

It's now been more than twenty years since that fateful day. Years of day-to-day routines have carved out a new normal. Now the cloud is subtler. Little signs of the grief cloud start to creep into my days. I get sluggish and sleepy. It's easier and easier to sit in the chair and watch TV or sleep much more than normal. I get impatient and irritable. Little things that normally wouldn't bother me get under my skin. I am tempted to just zone out and let the world pass me by. When I notice these tendencies, and look at the calendar, I make the connection. If it is close to December 5, I know the reason for this downward spiral.

Faced with these effects of grief, even after all these years, what do I do? How do I cope? While there is nothing wrong with remembering the day and feeling sad, I can't get stuck in feelings of self-pity or thoughts of what might have been. I have found some important things to focus on to help me get through the times when the cloud of grief rolls in.

One is to take care of my physical health. I need to make a concentrated effort to eat right, exercise, and drink plenty of water. While eating junk can provide a temporary emotional comfort, it is not good for my long-term health and well-being.

Another thing that helps during these times of sadness is to take some action to benefit some group or individual not connected to me. Pitching in to help some group or cause gets the focus off me. I never have to look far to find someone less fortunate that could use some help.

A gratitude list is a tool that is very helpful in adjusting my perspective, my attitude, and my mindset. I am blessed beyond measure. I have a safe, warm, comfortable home. I have loving parents and two beautiful daughters. I have an enjoyable, fulfilling job that makes a difference in people's lives. I have much to be thankful for. I have a caring, supportive church family. I have a constant companion in my Lord and Savior Jesus Christ. He has promised to never leave me or forsake me.

When I focus on the hope that I have in Christ, the cloud of grief and sadness dissipates. The light of Christ's mercy and grace pierces the darkness that threatens when I am reminded of the day my son died.

The promise of eternity free from sorrow and pain lifts my head and restores my joy.

> *He will wipe every tear from their eyes. There will be no more death or mourning or crying or pain, for the old order of things has passed away.* Revelation 21: 4

Michelle Ruddell

How Are Things Now?

It's been more than twenty-five years since Matthew died. In the first several years the pain was sharp. Tears came easily. I don't think I wore eye make-up for a year. As the years have passed, the happy memories seem to come to mind more quickly, and the sorrow, though present, is less sharp. Occasionally a song, a picture, or a memory will still sneak up on me and bring the tears.

I still think of him every day. I haven't forgotten my son. The difference is that now, most times, I think of him with a smile on my face and without a tear in my eye.

He will yet fill your mouth with laughter
and your lips with shouts of joy. Job 8:21

What Have I Learned?

Joy and sorrow are not mutually exclusive. It is possible to experience both simultaneously.

God is faithful. He will carry you through experiences you could not make it through on your own.

There are many, many parents who have experienced the death of a child. You are not alone in this grief.

However, the grief process is unique for each individual. It differs even for family members dealing with the same loss.

The old normal is gone. A new normal will take its place. Be patient with yourself while it unfolds.

Before Matthew died, I was afraid of lots of things. I feared making mistakes (although I made many). I was terrified that I wouldn't be able to deal with anything bad that would happen. I had no confidence in myself, and I assumed that my past mistakes had ruined any chance I ever had of being loved by God again.

A few years after my son was buried, I realized that fear was fading. I realized that God had carried me through the most difficult thing I would ever face. There was an odd sense of freedom in knowing that nothing worse could happen. My faith in God was renewed.

34

I gained a new understanding of God's gift to us in Jesus. He willingly endured the loss of his son for me and for you, so that we could be forgiven. Losing my own son gave new meaning to God's sacrifice.

Four years after the wreck, when I faced the escalation of domestic violence at the hands of my husband, I remembered how God had brought me through the worst thing I could ever imagine when Matthew died. That realization strengthened me to ask God for a way out, and He provided.

I don't know for sure, but I can't imagine me before the accident ever being able to even think about leaving that abusive marriage. I believe that knowing God had brought me through losing my child gave me the faith that he could also bring me through leaving my husband.

> *The LORD is my light and my salvation—*
> *whom shall I fear?*
> *The LORD is the stronghold of my life—*
> *of whom shall I be afraid?* Psalm 27:1

Passing It On

At some point you will transition from club newcomer to a member of the welcoming committee. There will be a time when you will encounter a friend or an acquaintance who has unwillingly joined our ranks. You will know the shock and the pain, yet you will also know strength and comfort. Your words won't take away their hurt, but they will bring comfort because you have been there.

It's difficult to know that nothing you can say will take away their pain. Your words can convey hope that life continues, and that joy will still be present.

I encourage you to reach out to those new to this group. The experience, though not easy, helps us as well as the newcomer. You may find yourself listening to the words you speak, realizing that you have come a long way and that you are making it through.

Yes, my soul, find rest in God;
my hope comes from him.
Truly he is my rock and my salvation;
he is my fortress, I will not be shaken.
My salvation and my honor depend on God.
He is my mighty rock, my refuge.

Made in the USA
Columbia, SC
16 February 2023

12108927R10022